Letters to the Sky

CAMELLIA STAFFORD was born in Warwickshire. She read English Literature and Language at King's College London and has an MA from The Courtauld Institute of Art. Her debut pamphlet *another pretty colour, another break for air* is published by tall lighthouse. Camellia divides her time between Warwickshire and London. *Letters to the Sky* is her first collection.

Letters
to the Sky

by

CAMELLIA STAFFORD

*For
Nia,

With Love,

Camellia

x   x   x*

SALT

CROMER

PUBLISHED BY SALT PUBLISHING
12 Norwich Road, Cromer, Norfolk NR27 0AX

Salt Publishing 2013

Printed in Great Britain by Berforts Information Press Ltd.

Typeset in Paperback 9 / 13

ISBN 978 1 907773 54 9 hardback

1 3 5 7 9 8 6 4 2

For My Darling Parents

Contents

Acknowledgements

I would especially like to thank Roddy Lumsden for his editorial finesse and belief in my work.

For their friendship, support and encouragement, I thank Annie Freud, Amy Key and Patrick Brandon.

Various poems included in *Letters to the Sky* were first published in my debut pamphlet *another pretty colour, another break for air* (tall-lighthouse, 2007).

Some of the poems or versions of them have appeared in the following publications: *Best British Poetry 2013* (Salt, 2013), *Penning Perfumes Volume II* (smashwords, 2013), *Follow the Trail of Moths* (Sidekick Books, 2013), *Oxford Poetry*, *Magma*, *The Pre-Raphaelite Review*, *Tate Etc.* and *Eyewear*.

For love, inspiration and the best times, thank you to my adored friends Claire, Gus, Han, Gerry, Amy, Antonio, John, Ruth, Sophie, Kath, Sarah, Tony, Steve and Glenn.

'the past falls open anywhere'

from *Black Ice and Rain*, MICHAEL DONAGHY

Letters to the Sky

"*Violet,*

before the surface of the lake slid over my head,
before my held breath eased its bubbles through water
and just before my arms recalled the butterfly stroke,
I like to think I saw you
                    lifted a cabinet's velvet veil
to peep at you like a painted miniature of a loved one
shielded from light. You were a watercolour baby –
all pale skin, eyes like blue suns setting in the dark
and a mouth like a giggling blossom
                    learning to take the air."

Before a mirror, I kneel to tend my face

Cache of gloss and brushes, gel and cake,
my make-up bag, ritually unzipped, reveals
silver encasements. Each bears use marks,
fingerprints of peachy foundation opalled
with tinct dusts, clouding the metallic shell.

Squat, in front of a cloudless looking-glass,
I vanish capricious shadows with a solution
of flesh, reliable in hue, coverage and set
by the powder pad's sweeps and presses
into every niche, tier and recess of my face.

Mantled with blusher, a silken brush swirls,
its powder blossoms flower on my cheeks.
Sponge applicator plunged through lustred
Cream strokes lips into a flittering glaze.
Candies perfume the next breath's confetti.

Possibilities of colour volunteer my eyes.
Lidded chamber of rose and aquamarine
shades tempt me with matte and shimmer.
I twirl my finger in their haloes applying
one, then another from the palette's rosary.

Corsage

How can a heart be broken like this,
when it's out of fashion to live for someone else.
Pop on another outfit, heart-shaped shades.
Step out into new love or Horatio Street,
where freshly watered hanging baskets
cry on your shoulder. It won't work.
You will discover the streets have turned
on you. Cremer St. cackling about the first date,
a blackish rose with gothic redolence.
Had you known the canker in that corsage,
would you have kept it on the windowsill,
set your heart afloat on the thought of it?
                  Drown a heart like this,
bury it under a silk bow between your breasts.
Focus on the pursuit of something useful.

Carousel

In the hall of mirrors her body is a wave, a zigzag.
All the freakish images of herself, the pier's elegant

antiquity soothes. An invitation to fare the sea on
a ribbon of architecture piques her fascination

with the seaside's heyday. She perceives herself
jollied along in a parade of tourists, holiday glad.

Her sailor dress frolics on the whip of the deep.
Toying with a new name for herself, a boyish one,

Frankie, she launches atop a wooden mare,
Dilys, whose painted eyes are rosette bright.

Frankie never fantasizes about the past, no bygone
day enchants her. A girl of the 1950s, if it came to it

she would ride her steed dauntlessly through a night
time storm, lightning could not crack her mettle.

She grips Frankie tightly, bobbed and spun, dizzied
by her foolhardy ways. The slowing of the ride

utters through their anatomies, the panorama stills.
Dilys halts her gallop in mid-air, organ notes close.

Stille Disco

How do you feel about this?
Each leaf above us shimmying,
a fragile wing of light and gloss,
each an echo of how my fingers sometimes quiver
or how my heart aches some mornings.

And, how do you see this?
Each dancer wearing headphones
to dance to music only he or she can hear,
each movement of an arm or leg
seeming with its energy to dispel the silence.

How does it seem to you?
Each painting hung on a wall of the museum
clamouring for your eyes to give it colour,
each casting you a story, emotion, none
or patiently waiting for someone's gaze.

How do you feel about anything?
The tallness of the houses here,
the steepness of the stairs,
the women wearing neon underwear in windows
or my hand as it slides into yours.

Two single beds pushed together
or a ride through the city perched
on the back of a bicycle, a piece of toast
with chocolate hundreds and thousands on
or me sitting in the Vondelspark asking:
how can I be any good at love until you are here?

Now

I knew that I must come outside
where ceilings ease into a reservoir of sky.
Even if the wind does lift the corners
of this page, unsettle my hair,
the words are here on the bee wing tips,
the confection of baby's breath.

It can be difficult to see the miniature
leaves of the rose plant, dots of clover
on the lawn. Abandon intrusive thoughts
for contemplation of the beech tree. Shade
of copper, branches labyrinthine, soothe me.

Now, I can write.

Figure with bindle

I see the antique figurine of you within the glass-fronted cabinet.
A young, fey fellow, legs washed in lilac, feet turquoise encased.

A bindle leant over your shoulder, inside its tied square of cloth:
your iPhone, copy of *The Heart is a Lonely Hunter*, a tenner, keys.

Your eyes appear constantly fixated on what lies ahead of you:
frilly landscape of hand-painted fans puddled with silver salvers.

A man's man, you prefer not to socialise with the ladies lounging
around on miniature china settees lapping up a sugar spoon view.

You close your ears to their prattling about the drawing room
antics, fantasise your escape to another showcase. Its curios

ideally gathered by a serious collector of rare coins and stamps,
sterling silver propelling pencils, ships in bottles, pre-1900s gilt

timepieces, tortoiseshell cigarette cases and oh, your cabinet wish
list is endlessly explicit but at the top, another fine figure of a lad,

who knows what it is to stand a century in emasculating legwear.
But wait! Cut the history! You've an incoming call on the iPhone.

Virginia Courtauld's Bathroom, Eltham Palace

A guest in your home, you are swell,
Virginia, to let me use your private suite.
Gold leaf becomes the complexion.
Water pours from the lion's mouth.
A dressing table drawer yields mimosa salts.

My own towel, it's only good form.
My bathing suit on, under my clothes.
Breathe deeply the aerial prosperity.
Close the door for privacy. Your pet lemur's
acquaintance I prefer to make later, over Bellinis.

Disrobe! Bath-side Psyche, marble cool,
observes me drift into a chimerical reverie.
The Courtauld's other visitors sail the ship-shape
rotunda of the adjoining art deco bedroom.
Imagine waking up to maple panelled walls!

*Next, on the tour, the unforeseen spectacle
of an aspirant Virginia bathing in a costume.*
I am sugar melting in a bain-marie,
Venus in the bassinet of an oyster shell,
a fire opal flickering in a dish of chalcedony,

a lotus opening in the heat,
Salome bewitching the rivulet, her underwater
adagios, an opaline Lalique poisson,
the pool softening my glass to flesh.
I am the air inside a bubble.

Liberty with Gerry

Your giggle bounces off the hydrangea mop-heads,
startling the peonies; you spring from ballet flat to ballet flat
and wave your arms to greet me like a ribbon dancer.

All Liberty's flowers revive in their buckets, straighten up
in ovation as if they have never viewed anyone so alive.
In the frisky cotillion of Great Marlborough Street, I'm your

dance partner. Impasse of traffic holds me back too long,
from crossing over to you. Our arms around one another!
We jitter from foot to foot. Freesias shimmy interpretively,

choreographing our delectation of each other. The girls,
who understand shopping, the artistry of looking, quick step
of conversation through the frisson of oak-panelled galleries.

Liberty prints ascend the tiers, revel in the timber's Tudor
revival. In the atrium, our thoughts are replaced by jewels.
Our mouths fall open. In Womenswear, I touch Lanvin.

Feathers run along my arms. Bubbles frothily titter in saucers.
A necklace of semi-precious stones, blue quartz and mother
of pearl, I hear the cabochon ask you: *May I have this dance?*

Out of peace of mind

Times, a peace touches down in me,
more gently than this sounds – less noticeably.
The tip of a honeyed spoon leaving my mouth
deposits a sap slipping south
with a fluency that couldn't have involved
a human hand. Surely angels are involved,
dipping the hems of their boy-white
gowns in the dewy float.

Then the tongues of dreams are with me.
I have the best of me – begin to be
without consciousness of anything
that might have been affecting
the easiness of being that should come,
now does come and I succumb,
relax into it like a child lulled in blankets,
life yet to slip out it secrets.

And then it gets so good
I think I'm through the unrest I should
have thought would wind its thorny cord
around my wrist, presenting its bleak reward
for living to wear as a bangle at every occasion.
I shouldn't have given in to the angels' persuasion.
For now all my armed thoughts come marching
through the harmony, their notes warring.

And Your Hair Is Devastating

Sometimes, a smudgy eye-line dirties your lower lashes,
a holographic suit is stretched over your compact body,
accentuating the cleanliest cornflower blue of your eyes.
A mirrorball onesie! I read your clothes can look wanky

unless you're very thin. Tonight, you're prettiest Pierrot,
a ruff of lacewings fluttering at your neck, tear-shaped
applique on your cheek. Accenting your smocked torso,
pom-poms. If we kiss, our lips will confect a new shade

of lipstick, pinky neon like the tutu worn by Old Gregg.
I'd kiss you with your webbed hands on, seaweed hair,
your just off-stage sweat slicking into face paint slippage.
But, I think I do prefer you in a floor length ermine fur.

Ah, when you twirl, its hem lifts like a cocktail umbrella
twiddling over the television screen. There is a casually
dressed you, teaming one sweet wrapper winkle picker,
silvered and skinny jeans, with one gold-sprayed bootie.

Your narratives are giddying you, are my comedic elixir.
A disorientated blue bottle, you buzz around the theatre,
switch faces with Dondy-lion. Be my superhero fantasia
man! Next, you're playing the part of a chocolate finger.

Daydreams: training as a hairstylist and becoming yours,
primping your mighty locks as thick as a Black Jack chew,
silky like an acrylic mix, mane of butterflies and feathers.
A resplendent hair artist, on all the tours, I'd go with you.

The Ruby in the Tree

There is my self-consciousness draped over the clouds.

Sunshine exposes it, transparently.

Look at my self-criticism bonded to the tarmac.

No wheels roll it out, only fix it in.

The ladybirds balance my frustration on their backs.

Their hard shells split to unleash the wings.

Disappointment is fused in condensation.

It veils the panes, obscures the garden views.

Anger is surreptitious, not clearly being anywhere.

The shock of a sudden sound heard in the night.

My desperation is the unknown creature.

It hustles through the leaves before the break of day.

The time I do not know who I am is 5 p.m. to 6 p.m.

I count the hour back to myself.

There is a ruby in the tree, my fascination.

In the early evening it sparkles blood orange.

March Display

I expected lily of the valley to blossom,
lemon centred pansies, narcissi,
and purple crocuses but they didn't.

Twilight came earlier. Flora buried
their heads in the bumpy soil, their petals
sullied by the earth's dark tint,

torn by the grain of the loam.
I worried at the birds' dysphoric calls.
The trees were not imperfect before.

Branches, an asymmetrical confusion,
twisted and looped around one another,
tried to find their space to grow.

The persistent kazoo hum of a shrunken
bodied bumble bee starved of nectar,
dizzy with paranoia, rang in my ears.

It was not the best Spring.
Sometimes the oddness of it made me
philosophical. The flowers upset me most.

Little Edie

Gloomy seductiveness of a Hampton's home in tatters,
sophistication run wild. Cats chased, racoons damned.
Talk of trousers worn under a skirt: provides the option
to remove the skirt for use as a cape. Mother daughter
spats over dress sense, the cruelty of Big Edie sending
her daughter's only beau away. Little Edie's fantasies:
a Libran suitor, escape to *"any little rat-hole in New York."*

Offbeat, the gramophone accompanies their sing-song
of tea time hits from when they lived in the pink. High
notes peel from the walls. Lavish remnant, a gardenia
panel of wall paper displayed poster-like above the bed.
Little Edie's lifelong dream: to be a great dancer. Black
leotard and pantyhose outline her body's rousing march.
Playful smiles, she spangles stars and stripes in her hand.

On being told you used to be amazing

I dip into a clutter of fashion

earrings, the kind that are plastic painted gold,

try to explain I'm still the same person, domino

a thrift of cowboy boots.

Once the talking is over, pictures settle:

waiting to meet someone on High Holborn,

shoulders bare to the night, halter-necked

neck curled for a kiss.

Idealized for bright shoes

clicking by The Serpentine, Australian brown

dress, a thing for history of art.

Here I am, wondering if what I was told

was true, a vintage cardigan hanging

from my frame, a yearning for bittersweet days,

a thing for nothing. Here, I am . . .

Echo 2   7 Romeo Uniform

The neighbourhood's plants we identified still wear a glaze
of our walking conversations. I could track the forgettable,
the ups, failures, the times celebratory in their demeanours,
by the inclination of a stem, frilled edge of a crinoline leaf.

We began talking at a party, sitting side by side on a floor
in a house in Haringey, two hilarious just-out-of-teens.
We were possessed: you, a boy of lime green expression to
my 60s lilac girl, unknowing of the things we would outlast.

Remember summers, the garden you created, extra chamber
of our house, housed mallow, yellow courgettes. Cherries
wrapped in glass ripened beside me. On the lounger, in love-
in-a-mist ink I wrote letters to the sky, the open windows.

Away

Seems to you I have fallen out of the world,
for I am a hundred miles away in a land
where car journeys unveil a rove of pylons
through the fields' green and yellow mosaic.
I could follow their bowed wires home-home,
over the farmsteads, the *Two Hoots* stable.

Here, lanterns pearl their daytime respite.
Hedgehog scuttles the lawn where I sailed
the boat of my climbing frame, swung flight
from twists of orange rope and lined snap-
dragons freckled with pebble ground pollen
across the slab to trade on my lawn travels.

You're right, I have fallen out of the world,
for I am a hundred miles away in a land
where someone gives me every meal
and the clothes I brought with me are clean
as a glint of silver by the time I say *goodbye*
in the home-home voice I keep from the world.

Diorama

In dreams of other lives, I have lived.
Should I venture to altitudes figured,

the mystery would be in how to get
there, not in how to be once there.

Loiter on the fringes of make-believe,
observe myself adroitly poised, hand

at rest on a man's knee. I watch her,
this me, thrive through mise-en-scène,

name the clouds with her daughter,
multiple rainbows doubling in the sky.

Parasol of confidence chaperones her.
Its sunny material bestows her favours.

She belongs here more than anyone,
so how can I join in with her? Say,

she caught me peering into scenes from
her meaningful life, would she mistake

my hopes for a far flung ruse,
not help me to take my place?

Fortune

Not a day to write of unhappiness
but to wake in palomino rays,

to discover the carved ormolu shell
held to my ear does croon ocean sounds,

to notice the laden trees' glowing pears
inspired the invention of the light bulb,

red apples evolved the paper lantern,
ripening plushly, the trees enlightened,

to know the word of the day is cosmology,
to read Zelda Sayre wore a nude swimsuit

to give the impression of skinny-dipping.
Impossible not to think of a lapping bay,

forecast an amiable current in the water.

Staying in to wash my hair

So, to prepare the basin,
ensure it's temperately composed,
protective of strands to be grown.

Check the tank's coppered dome,
smarts of heat. Fervent waters
flow clairvoyant resources,

prophesies of where else I'd be…
Turn down a city's summer's eve.
My orange childhood pouring cup,

readied for rinsing. Open window
exposes a plane of mulberry dusk,
discordant with the bathroom's

uncompassionate fluorescence.
Antique breeze, lavender trespass.
Exterior of indoor world,

intrudes my inner existence.
True, I had wanted to live my life.
Christen lukewarm water,

aluminium snowfall liquefies
in the sink's half-moon
of self-preservation.

December

My identity skates right past me.
Let her go!
Surrender her to the blanched ice.
If I do not stop trying to be someone,
I will never learn who I am.

Summer, waters flowed.
No river or lake froze over.

She stayed with me, I her lady in waiting.
On the mirror she wrote choices,
intentions. I polished them away,
entreated myself to discover nothingness.

There are no answers,
only my attempts to find them.

When she returns to me,
I will take her back, changed, un-changed.
For now, winter's earlier nightfall
accords me a hiding place.
In the dark it matters less
who she is or I am.

Chattertoniana

By his bed, a small leaded window
opens onto distant roofs. The drear spire
of a Shoreditch church perforates the sky.
Scant of nature, one potted plant on the sill
dwarves the buildings to a toy town.

Peaceful as he looks at rest on the bed
in trousers of lapis lazuli to the shin,
white stockings rippled, slightly soiled
from walks amid the toy town alleys,
I want to lift his hand that dangles
its last touch of the seen world,
from the floor of the tiny attic room.

Where his poison drowsy head slipped
from the yellowed bolster, I'd scoop it
upon my lap, nurse its artful talents there,
running my fingers through the flame
of his hair until I am seared by romance.

She thinks of her dresses

Cool, still, suspended from their rail:
lace at rest, a skirt of chiffon. Cinch
of silk loosed from the dent of her waist,
draped with the others in stasis too long.

She recalls the twirling of a flared mini,
a floodlit evening, the garden of strange,
unclassified flowers and the feel of his hair,
wavy, almost familiar.

There's satin of palest apple green,
stroked with hawthorn leaves, recollection
of quivering hands before an audience,
a room of friends.

In frillery, prettiest of all her dresses,
the rose and butterfly halter-neck survived
without a hurt or snag, whilst an earring fell
and he roughed her hair, a fuss of platinum.

One is stiller than the others, without a story,
sedate and saved for the right occasion.
She wishes the silk to narrate a new tale,
fresh page, fashion plate, verse of rebirth.

Needlepoint

When we first met it drugged the air,
sent skies scarlet, the moon lime green.
There was no possibility of moving,
without my movement piercing through
a consciousness of yours designed by me.

You noticed everything: my heels like spurs
needling the flesh of Hackney Road,
your name embroidered on my underskirt,
the thread of cream stitching lip to lip
when in the patisserie, I giggled.

Colour

Flower heads wander the river water's violet
surface, their petals' wetted pinks and reds
rocking in the water cot where the posy
landed when it was thrown, uncaught.

The sun flushes a greying bridge curving
across the river, glazing the ashy tone
of its wood with a caramel lustre, smiling
upside down at the blue, blue cloud-scuffed sky.

Fields surround, bristling their green
and yellow needles, shadowing under the shape
of a white plane passing over the flower-kinked
river drowning endlessly in itself.

Floridaflora

Listen, the plants are telling us their names:
calliopsis, zinnia, ginger lily, lantana, blue anise, aster,
button willow, camellia, cherokee rose, ixora, mistflower,
moonflower, pink purselane, gay feather, seaside oxeye.

We pick up the language of *beebalm, maypop,*
black-eyed susan, american blue heart, blue forked curls,
loblolly bay, sweet pepperbush, air potato, fiddlewood,
shoebutton ardisia, downy milkpea, oleander, coco plum.

Our tongues slop heavy with heat, and drowsy.
To fall asleep, we reel off: Georgia, South Dakota,
Alabama, Oregon, Iowa, Oklahoma, Vermont, Louisi . . .
We rest on The Panhandle, what we wished for

tossed in dimes to the floor of the Citrus Tower.
Our lives, simple, our breaths held in fruitcups.
Breakfast from the orange groves: *navel, honeybell,*
dancy, temple, orlando tangelo, hamlin, valencia, fallglo.

Halloween Lane

Come with me down Halloween Lane,
your face painted snowdrop white.
My eyes masked with black lace. A gown
beneath your blazer, sneak out of class.
The teacher's eyes are blackboard dim.
Think, how coffee will seem rebellious
when we break from vintage trawling.
Let our hair be sapphire on a cobbled street.

You, are the girl I have been looking for.
Let's drip with glamour, our evening wear
in the afternoon. Sing to me of pillbox hats
and sorority. Be careful sweetheart
of the man with a poorly face, wince
of his open sore. Bear him no ill, only take
my arm, skitter over the cobblestones,
through the boutiques of yesteryear.

Karaoke in Bow

East and retro in tea dresses,
lads skulked off, left us the empty dance floor,
a forecast of songstresses and pop.

Flanked by local teens and their mothers,
we danced the way of girls who begin friendships
with dancing and duets.

No, you can't hurry it
but our Saturday night rendition of 'Jolene'
to a pub full of strangers linked us.

Vulnerability did too. I cried and you fell.
The contents of your handbag fanned out into the road.
Tiny beads of blood collected on your knees

like precious gems; a shared taxi,
promised us to one another's confidences.

Evelyn and Aurora Triumphans

Evelyn, in her Chelsea studio cultures a goddess, Aurora,
paints her skin with pearls ground by pestle and mortar.

She works the canvas, snaking Aurora's body in circlets
of rope and crooks her neck to stroke in detailed anklets.

Her romantic feeling for William De Morgan flourishes
as she smooths the deity's physique with her brushes.

Channelling the dawn crossing Manresa Road, she recasts
the silvered city into a flinty mythical landscape. Contrasts,

she mixes reds, carmine and carnelian, applies Slade-
honed techniques to tones she hopes will never fade

on angels' wings. Announcing Aurora's victory of quelling
night, the heavenly host cock their trumpets, dispelling

darkness with a fanfare. Evelyn's mother openly despairs
of her wish for a daughter not an artist. Via the overtures

of her uncle John Roddam Spencer Stanhope in Florence,
Evelyn falls for Botticelli. Immersed in the Renaissance,

missing the Florentine sun, she wanders the chilly galleries
of The Uffizi. She is restless, energetic. Her sensitivities

are, according to her elder sister, Wilhelmina, excessive.

Respite

Gardenias fall from a chiffon sky into my lap.
I lift the corners of my crocheted apron skirt
and convey my scented bounty to the stream
where pebbles of blue quartz laze on the bed.
I arrange my flowers along the banks, myself
upon the grass and repose as they sing to me,
alluring canticles of their unexpected desires.

In conversation with myself

Hours I disappear into the folds
of incessant fabric,
my hands out-stretched
as if walking through
an unfamiliar house in darkness.

Repeatedly, the same things are
in the crevices, disused bells
bound in glass, a caged duplicate
of whichever room I am in.
The staircases have frail banisters,
breath taking inclines.

Perched on a windowsill,
my back to the sky's amethyst,
I tell myself, *this isn't me.*

Aisles

Cream flustered me
I faltered in Condiments
Swooned in Eggs

In Detergents my heart palpitated
Pulse raced in Bread
In Foil I couldn't breathe

At the Delicatessen my vision blurred
I felt strangled in Ready Meals
Nearly abandoned my basket

And then I thought *Fuck It*
I'm not dying in Tesco

En route

If you want to hear music
en route you have to sing,
in this ramshackle-beautiful
flying-machine of mine.

A slew of cereal boxes,
spray-painted, glue-gunned:
a Chrysler building, carriage
of the London Eye hybrid.

She has three sets of wings:
one paper, a foil, one pink,
and plastic cup headlamps
lit with highlighter pen.

Her steering wheel's a fancy
hatbox lid. With a cellophane
cone of marshmallows for
a horn, she alerts air-traffic.

I sit a little nervously
inside her wavering walls,
take off from the narrow
runway of crazy-paving.

I never think of landing,
safely or at all as she whisks
a frosting of icing-trails
through a pretend sky.

I suppose

You, a fuzzy edged soul that night, spoke

of dining with gangsters and ate a fairy cake whole,

the way men I admire do.

Pleas were ineffective, mired to high table,

you.   I'm not even sure why I wanted you to dance.

Perhaps some remnant of an easy time

when you showed me how to do the mashed potato.

Please describe in the space below why you are applying for the role of Museum Assistant at The Wallace Collection

I have extensive experience of dressing in fanciful outfits, a contemporary take on eighteenth century ensembles, inspired by the peony robed lady of Fragonard's *The Souvenir*, combined with my highly developed interpersonal skills.

Although, I specialised in the Young British Art Movement, the current trend is all a little too edgy for me. A recent trip to The Saatchi, virtually pornographic. I prefer the tamer, subtler effects of titillation discreetly depicted in *The Swing*.

I am a co-operative team worker with a great admiration for Oliver Peyton's café and am keen to assist my colleagues in the taking of afternoon tea. For example, I successfully savoured the Parisian Tea accompanied by champagne.

There is no doubt, I would have hit it off with Watteau, empathising with great talent going unrecognised in one's lifetime. A committed and reliable employee, my career history speaks for itself. Best not to contact my referees

prior to the interview, I would prefer not to be upstaged by their glowing testimonies of me. My love of miniatures, especially those by Augustin, stems from my passion for studying my face in a compact mirror. A reflective thinker,

I spend time both in and outside of work in contemplation.
As with the Dutch painter Gerrit Dou, it takes me hours
to achieve anything. The dust must settle before I begin.
The results of my work, like his, are those of a perfectionist.

The Archeress

Take your stance. Faultlessly streamlined,
the longbow with your body, string drawn
fluently to the corner of your mouth, taut
with aim, the sight flush with your open eye.
August in alignment, confident in purpose,
you reiterate Artemis, in the field of men.

Before you loose the arrow, doubtlessly
to shoot the tip into the black or gold,
the men murmur: *let's see how it's done.*
May I fix you in that graceful pose,
tell you, a love of trees, your childhood's
wood-dwelt dreams are not coincidences?

Certain, a warrior, you were never more
at home than here. Present environ fades.
In its stead a wooded enclave becomes you,
tunic of drapery enclothes you. Straighten,
your fingers, let your arrow glide by lime,
horse chestnut, silver birch, oak, aspen.

Elizabeth Bay

for Glenn

It is my fancy the seabed is where you now sleep,
wake and float back up to a paradisiacal surface,
are salted, beachy, caramelised in gorgeous living.

Coves take the minutes of our nostalgic meetings.
They scribble your change of address on the tide.
So the harbour bridge is visible from your studio.

You dine on the marina, barramundi, red snapper.
On Google Earth, I dream I spot you sunning on
your balcony. A skyline of distant buildings shade

your crown like different styles of hats protecting
you from the heat, perhaps. You will never burn
under the rays, having been conceived by the sun.

Sunday

I had been longing to see you
find you squeezing my arm through the crowds
to register you in the 'o' of 'hello'
whatever's happened to your hair
lain flat against your head as if you have hardly been living
as if I care about hair as I take your soul
into my arms   into myself
holding it there as if this could be
for the last and I must let you know as every remnant
of coffee in every paper cup pooling
in the shallows of a Brick Lane kerb reheats
and every brown bag smeared
with the grease of salt beef puffs up
my god it's good to see you
scraggy in your moonlit pink suit
more vulnerable   more beautiful
than ever before but also you look
terrible and you are someone
I love *really love* and since you were made for it   unquestionably
I hope you get to be great

I will stay at home and talk on the telephone

It's tricky to explain what I'm up to these days,
whose dawns snap like the polystyrene cups
I cracked to seed beads in the King's cafeterias,
as you checked my pulse and said things like,
today, your aura is apricot.

I am hidden at the end of the last ring
before I pick up. My voice transpires over
a battery. I stay at home and talk of hem
lengths, paper bouquets to my faraway sister.
Toy with the idea you will call me

from the pay phone at your old shared house,
Turnpike Lane, knelt on the floor by a blot
of silvers and coppers, satisfying sounds
of their clatter through our powwows,
when we said things like, *paradiso e inferno!*

Many late nights, you fell asleep on the line,
after hours of talking in the bar, the library,
our apres-class jinks around Covent Garden.
I never hung up but sometimes I woke you.
Others, I stayed quiet.

Dear Camden

Zillions of plastic butterflies spun transparencies
in a window that gave me sky, perfect tenements,
a church steeple. A dolls house flat, we reached
our hands in, to brush cameo adornments onto
bric-a-brac, the chest of drawers we hauled back,
a fold-down table gleaned from a willing mews.

Something shone or flew in or out of everything.
Ash flicks in a range of trays, a teal glass swan,
the peach retro swivel one, aquamarine kidney
shaped, tin foil coaster sorts appropriated in cafes.
Bubbles streamed from your casement, a machine
you bought, frothing over court entrance steps.

Iridescent aerial spheres glissaded all the York
Way up. Our overly posh belligerent neighbour
ticked us off in his seeming sole attire, a dressing
gown. Characters surrounded us. Often wailing,
'the woman' woke me, from her regular seat, wall
beneath my window, strange music to my naivety.

Camden's town gripped me in a clinch. I picked up
fashion on the streets. Pavements inclined to soften,
tilt for my platform heeled feet, swore their oaths
to me as I swore myself to them. Their alcoholic
devotees welcomed me in. Cries, I heard one night
heralded bouquets: *I'll miss you sleeping in my doorway.*

Whoosh! Courtyard fountains, Somerset House
completed me. I overdosed on Emin, Starr, Landy,
in a coveted window seat in the library. My much
seen DVD, Derek Jarman's *Jubilee*, I trilled: *my love
is like a red, red rose* . . . thought I got situationism
but it was all Guy Debord to me! I worked instead

on pseudonyms, copied Cosey Fanni Tutti's style.
I was friends with Lacey Gusset, the friend of Cyril
Disobedience, friend of The Lady of the Asphyxias.
I referenced Bananaman in my dissertation bound
in claret leather, discoursed on the use of personal
possessions in Starr's *Hypnodreamdruff* installation.

Zillions of plastic butterflies spun for an only child.
My cookery book was named *How to Cook*. Teatime,
our culinary flops advanced from the serving hatch.
My careless taste buds were tastefully overwhelmed
by other sweetnesses of freedom, evening parlour
games: contortion of our bodies struggling through

the hatch like a cat flap, teddy bears' cyber discos.
No heating, we cloaked in blankets, you modelled
yours royally, looked like a model anyway. Sashay
the fleece, I called you *my Lord*, played the peasant.
In other roles we created the parts of Darling and
Vivian, amusing one another with our posh accent.

Dabbling in studded cuffs n collars, bell bottoms,
lamé, lurex, dip-dyed anything, nighties for dresses.
Our Johnnos Clarkos round ours, camera on a strap,
emerged triple-belted, sunnies blue flowered from
pillaging your clothes rail then mine. Why not dress
up, take a photographic road trip over Delancey

Street, up to Kentish Town, pose before a triptych
of well painted garage doors? Local piss air seeped
into the photographs, your expressions. Backdrop:
a frieze of graffiti, our scowly turn of the century
looks, giggle burst grimaces popped deliriousness.
On the kerb opposite Our Lady Help of Christians,

I perched, my for-a-frock-negligee gutter hemming.
Plastic and marabou tiara, left over from Christmas,
its little girlish agenda, nativity play prettiness, sired
a dinky spire atop my head. From my anthology
of Italian beaded handbags, the topaz, cherished
in my lap, laid ajar, a dollar note from Clarko's trip

to New York within. He captured me. I journalled
minutiae into the night, curtain-less glass granting
the companionship of tenement bulbs winking on,
off, the heavens conveyed helicopters batting lashes,
my still, loyal steeple. Diaries quoted excerpts from
conversations, recorded chatter celebrated for being

momentous. Belief was mine, when I was not aware
of it. *Oh my god, oh my god*, my face was in my hands.
By chance at the garage, I met the boy from school,
a natural artist, who drew my profile in GCSE art.
Trouble, I knew it and we hid in the bathroom, *woo
hoo, woo hoo*, he called through our dolls house door

nightly for a week. Could he have been a balanced
boy? But none of them were, in those days, for me.
The sculptor admitted his heroin habit early on,
the photographer was a stalker. Sleeping in a single
bed, I fell in love with other things, see through
umbrellas, a Jeffrey Eugenides novella; one or two

male friends, in purity, I loved from afar. My lust
for the market was perhaps averse to love. Fishnet
popsocks, bright leg warmers – the paraphernalia
of an *Electric Ballroom* girl. PVC would have been
a step too far. Leather-trousered, the gothically
presented man in the emporium of PVC took me

upstairs. A locked storeroom, where *all the best all
in ones*, apparently were kept. Realising my mistake,
I fled, accused by the owner of not getting London.
Zillions of plastic neon butterflies span their effects,
my comforters in an hour of vulnerability, a mobile
in a nursery. I was spellbound back to calmness.

Saturday – my day of work in the decorative arts.
Asleep, alone in the office, in my boss' armchair,
I awoke to the sound of the door's dingle dongle,
sprang up like a ballerina in a child's jewellery box.
De Morgan tiles were de rigeur for the clientele,
those depicting ducks or fish, the most popular.

A regular kept tossing all his cigarette ends in urns,
another would drop in, in ill-fitting shorts for a chat
on his morning runs, quite the charmer. Phone calls
from my boss began *anything happening?* I prepared
a range of answers to his mantra question but never
knew what was going on. Nothing had a price on.

Dear Camden, you had a rival in Portobello, only
a dalliance, my bit on the side. Her macaroon terrace
selections floridly appealed but she didn't quite get
your shanty idyllicism. The 390 always brought
me back to home, any infidelity soon forgotten, took
a wander in Dolly Rockers, detected myself forgiven.

We blu-tacked faux carnations to the walls, bleached
the washing up basin to igloo white, sprayed the toilet
silver. My overspill of clothes queued up the hallway.
A montage of photos was stippled with grease spots
opposite the tinkly stove. We reached our hands into
our dolly's kitchen, made toast, tea in plastic crockery.

In a window that gave me sky, the perfect tenements, a church steeple, butterflies spun transparencies. Hues of neon light-catchers twirling through the chronicles of a daydream existence. In pursuit of air, I flung open the sash, zillions flew out into the streets of Camden Town, where I lived, loved in my life's fair perfection.